Thrift Savings Plan:

A Practical Guide to the TSP

By

Kirk G. Meyer

Thrift Savings Plan: A Practical Guide to the TSP by Kirk G. Meyer

Thrift Savings Plan:

A Practical Guide to the TSP

Copyright © 2014 by Kirk G. Meyer

Why I Wrote this eBook

If you are like me, you work for the government or are the spouse of someone who works for the government, and no one explained the Thrift Savings Plan or TSP to you. I do not know about your agency, but mine does not explain the TSP to anyone, be that a new hire or a seasoned employee. No one is in the human resource office to answer even the most basic TSP question. And let's face it, if you are a FERS employee, the TSP will play a significant role in your retirement. While this eBook is not an all-encompassing reference for the TSP, it addresses many of the essential things you need to know about the TSP.

Why You Should Buy this eBook

Again, as I stated in the previous section, agencies do a terrible job explaining the TSP, how it works, how important it is to your retirement, or how to make changes to your TSP account. This eBook goes into those details to help you understand the TSP, its importance, and how to manage your TSP account to a degree. This eBook makes up for some of the shortfalls of various agencies when it comes to the employee and explaining the TSP's inner workings. That is where Thrift Saving Plan: A Practical Guide to the TSP comes in handy.

Thrift Savings Plan: A Practical Guide to the TSP by Kirk G. Meyer

My GIFT to You!

As a big thank you for getting Thrift Savings Plan: A Practical Guide to the TSP, I want to offer you valuable gifts and a chance to get some on-going financial advice. Just for getting this book, it entitles you to my Budget Spreadsheet and Debt Reduction Spreadsheet I usually sell for $10. It is yours free for getting Thrift Savings Plan: A Practical Guide to the TSP and signing up for my free email newsletters that have previews to my eBooks. These special articles are geared towards personal finance and now access to these two useful spreadsheets. To get your spreadsheets now, simply go to my blog's website and sign up today. Visit http://bit.ly/KGMLetter to get your free valuable spreadsheets.

Table of Contents

Thrift Savings Plan: A Practical Guide to the TSP by Kirk G. Meyer

Introduction

The Thrift Savings Plan or TSP is a retirement benefit of US federal government employees similar to private employers' 401(k) plans. The TSP is open to all federal employees and uniformed service members and designed as a long-term savings plan utilized for retirement. And like private 401(k) plans, the TSP is offered as a Traditional TSP or the newer ROTH TSP. The original TSP was first created by Congress in 1986, evolving over the years to resemble what federal employees and uniformed service members can utilize for their retirement today.

Some advantages of the TSP over that of traditional 401(k) plans and individual retirement accounts are that it boasts some of the lowest fees of any investment offered to federal employees, uniformed service members, or the investing public. While at first, it may appear that the TSP does not offer enough options for a plan participant to diversify, that could not be further from the truth. Like many private 401(k) plans, the federal government offers an agency match for Federal Employees Retirement System (FERS) employees.

Thrift Savings Plan: A Practical Guide to the TSP by Kirk G. Meyer

Compounded over one's entire career, the TSP combined with retirees' pension annuity and social security supports one's retirement from the federal government.

Since August of 2010, all new FERS employees have been enrolled in the TSP by default. As a new employee, the participant's agency has started the TSP with a 3% automatic contribution of the participant's base salary. This is besides the 1% automatic agency contribution, and the 3% is matched 100% by the agency. The fourth and fifth percentage of the participant's base salary contributed to the TSP. It is matched 50% on each dollar. At a minimum, a FERS employee should contribute the initial 5% to take full advantage of the agency's matching program. After the TSP account is created, a participant may access the account through the TSP's website at www.tsp.gov.

Any participant may elect to have funds invested in a Traditional TSP or the newer ROTH TSP. In 2014 a participant may elect to contribute up to $17,500, and participants over the age of 50 are allowed an additional $5,500 in catch-up contributions. Regardless of how a participant elects to have contributions treated, the agency matched funds. The automatic 1% agency contribution is allocated to a Traditional TSP since taxes have not been paid on those funds as on the ROTH TSP funds. The treatment of a participant's contributions will be examined in much more detail in that section of the booklet. It may be best to consult a financial planner or tax expert before determining how a participant should elect to treat their contributions.

The maintenance of a participant's TSP can simply be done on the TSP website. The site allows for many options, such as re-allocation of assets between funds or inter-fund transfers. It will also allow a participant to change the asset allocation between the TSP's ten funds. The site is also the location where a participant can initiate any loans taken out against the TSP value. If the participant needs to find forms used in the proper maintenance of the TSP account, also found on the TSP website. Like many 401(k) plans, the TSP allows for transferring retirement assets into the TSP plan, provided they meet the plan's guidelines. It is also similar to other retirement accounts in that the TSP is passed to heirs by using a beneficiary designation.

An in-depth review will be conducted on each of the plan's ten funds. In this review, examine the fees associated with the fund, as will its volatility and some risks associated with each. There are two bond funds, three equity funds, and five lifecycle funds designed similarly to target dated mutual funds. The booklet will also discuss diversifying within the five main funds and how, by combining them, a participant can increase potential returns by reducing volatility and risk.

Finally, we will examine the different methods and ways a participant can access or withdraw the TSP funds. The plan offers a fairly diverse group of methods that one can use to access the funds that have accumulated in the TSP over the participant's career. The booklet will also conclude with an overview of the death benefit of the TSP and how it affects the beneficiary or surviving heir to the account.

Overview of the TSP

The ability to participate in the TSP is available to all federal civilian employees and uniformed service members. The TSP is the government's version of a private employer's 401(k) plan aimed at long-term savings for retirement. Like 401(k) plans, the TSP is a defined contribution plan. The amount in the retirement account is determined by the employee's contribution, any agency match, and the portfolio's return. Congress established the TSP with the Federal Employees' Retirement System Act of 1986, thereby creating the Federal Employees' Retirement System or FERS. FERS replaced the Civil Service Retirement System, or CSRS, similar to a uniformed service member's retirement system.

Some distinct advantages to saving for retirement in the TSP is deposits are made through automatic payroll deductions. This is advantageous in saving for retirement because the funds are deposited in the participant's TSP account without them having to do anything. Some of the most effective savings methods are set up for automatic deposits where nothing is done on the participant's part. And any time we do not have to write a check for our retirement accounts and have it taken directly from our paychecks before it is seen makes for a very effective savings mechanism.

While the TSP only offers ten investment choices, they are a diversified group of investment options, especially when accounting for the lifecycle funds. While many people who invest for retirement use traditional accounts or ROTH accounts, the TSP allows for either or a combination of the two. Done pre-tax , Traditional TSP contribution with all of the earnings growth on a tax-deferred basis. On the other hand, it is a ROTH TSP, where the funds are contributed on a post-tax basis, with all gains and proceeds being tax-free when withdrawn. If a participant receives any matching funds, they must by law be placed in the Traditional TSP portion of the account, as these funds have not been taxed, so any funds and their proceeds will be taxed when withdrawn.

TSP funds have extremely low administrative and expense fees compared to mutual funds and even most exchange-traded funds that offer similar investment choices and assets. The maximum expense fees are 0.039% or less, which equates to $0.39 or less per $1,000 invested for all ten of the TSP's funds, including the semi-actively managed lifecycle funds. Low fees, combined with employees covered by the FERS system, will receive a match, make contributions to the TSP essential for a participant's retirement. Most agencies will match the first 3% dollar for dollar, and the 4th and 5th% matched at fifty cents on the dollar. That means, at a minimum, a TSP participant should contribute at least 5% of his or her salary to receive the maximum matching benefit.

FERS employees use the TSP as part of their basic retirement to go along with their FERS basic annuity and social security benefits. For those covered under the CSRS system or uniformed services, the TSP is used to supplement their annuity, since CSRS employees do not receive social security. As CSRS employees, they receive a much higher annuity payment in place of a Social Security benefit. So, their contributions to the TSP will not receive the agency matching as FERS employees will. Regardless of one's retirement classification, the TSP can and will increase every government employee's retirement assets. As with any successful retirement account, the key is to start as soon as possible and allow compound interest to work for the participant. The difference between an account that is active for 20 years compared to the same account that is active over a 30- or 40-year period is amazing. Depending on the participant's contributions and returns, the balances at the end of the 30 years and 40-year period can be four times the amount in the 20-year account. For example, a $5,500 investment made today with a return of 6% annually will grow to $17,639 in 20 years, and that same investment would grow to $56,571 in 40 years. That is the power of compounding interest.

Starting a TSP Account

All FERS employees will have a 1% automatic agency contribution applied to their retirement annuity regardless of when hired. For FERS employees hired after July 31, 2010, their agency automatically enrolled them in the TSP, contributing 3% of their basic pay, automatically invested in the G-Fund (discussed later). If, when hired, a different percentage of basic pay was elected to be contributed to the TSP account, that amount will override the agency's automatic 3% contribution. A participant who contributes the full 5% will receive the full agency match, resulting in 10% of the participant's salary in savings after agency matching, and considered the automatic 1% agency contribution.

For those FERS employees hired before August 2010 who did not elect to contribute to the TSP, they still have an account that will contain the automatic 1% agency contribution for their annuity—investing these funds in the TSP's G-Fund by default. Again, it is wise to contribute 5% of one's basic pay to receive the agency's matching program's full benefit. The agency that the employee works for will dictate how they may enroll in the TSP program. Some agencies will allow participants to sign up, change election percentages, or the TSP's tax treatment through websites such as www.employeeexpress.gov. For agencies not set up through sites such as Employee Express, make enrollment and changes through the agency's human resources department. All TSP contributions must be set up for CSRS and uniformed service members through the agency's preferred method. And as a reminder, CSRS and uniformed service members will not receive an agency match on their contributions.

As a new FERS employee, one should put a great deal of consideration into making at least the full 5% contribution of basic pay to gain the full benefit of the agency match. Once established a TSP contribution election, the TSP participant should look for their TSP account number and www.tsp.gov password in the mail, and their ThriftLine Personal Identification Number (PIN). Once a new participant has received his login materials, he can go into his TSP account and determine what fund or funds to invest. This is done on the TSP website, and the participant determines the percentage allocated to each asset class. TSP participants can also log into TSP's website to make inter-fund transfers, which may be limited, depending on what TSP funds are involved in the transfer.

As a new employee, it is also a good time to name a beneficiary of the TSP account in the event of the participant's death. This is a good move to keep the TSP assets out of the participant's probate estate; it is also a good estate planning tool. But the main reason for naming a beneficiary is to ensure that the participant's wishes are carried out at his or her death.

Contributions and Tax Treatment

There are two main categories of contributions in a TSP, and they are employee contributions made under FERS, CSRS, or uniformed service members, and the agency match for FERS employees. Now a TSP participant may contribute up to $19,500 into a TSP account in 2020, and those participants over the age of 50 may contribute an additional $6,500 as a catch-up contribution. To qualify for catch-up contributions for those participants over the age of 50, they must first have contributed the maximum of $19,500. TSP participants must also decide if they would like a Traditional TSP, a ROTH TSP, or a combination of the two. A TSP participant may elect to contribute, for example, half of their contributions to a ROTH account and half to a Traditional account. With the FERS employee's agency match and automatic 1% contributions, it is always placed in the Traditional TSP account. Under section 415(c) of the Internal Revenue Code (IRC) established that the annual additions limit, which is the dollar amount of all contributions (Traditional, ROTH, tax-exempt, and all agency contributions), has a maximum of $57,000 for 2020. This limit is set annually by the Internal Revenue Service (IRS).

For a Traditional TSP contribution, the funds are taken from the participant's base pay before withholding any taxes or after taxes with a ROTH TSP. The percentage of the participant's base pay is deducted from each pay period automatically for regular FERS employees. These deductions are then sent directly to the TSP plan administrator for investment and followed until the participant gives directions to change the percentage of base salary to be saved, stop contributions altogether, or reach the plan limits, and contributions can no longer be made.

Thrift Savings Plan: A Practical Guide to the TSP by Kirk G. Meyer

Uniformed service members can also contribute a percentage of their base pay to the TSP plan; however, they may also contribute between 1% and 100% of incentive pay, special pay, or bonus pay, provided a participant contributes at least 1% from basic pay. Once the plan limits are met, no further TSP contributions will occur. Uniformed service members may elect to contribute any special pay even if they are not currently receiving the special pay. If the participant does receive these special payments, contributing the allotted percentage to their TSP account. If a uniformed service member receives tax-exempt combat pay, the classification of the funds is vital. If the participant places the funds in a Traditional TSP, taxing the proceeds upon withdrawal. If placing any in a ROTH TSP, when withdrawn tax-free, provided certain criteria are met, this section will be discussed later.

Remember, TSP participants over the age of 50 and have contributed the maximum allowed are eligible to contribute an additional $6,500 as a catch-up contribution. While a catch-up contribution is voluntary, done in either a Traditional or ROTH TSP. To be eligible for catch-up contributions, the participant must first contribute an amount that will enable the participant to reach the maximum contributions limit by the end of the year in the year they turn 50. A participant may elect to make catch-up contributions to the TSP account. Once a participant has reached the regular and catch-up contribution level limits, all contributions to the participant's TSP will end, or it will end at the end of the calendar year provided both thresholds have not been met. Catch-up contributions must have a new election each year and will not continue from year to year. For uniformed service members, catch-up contributions may not be made from the special payments. If a participant is in a catch-up position and receives tax-exempt pay, those funds may only be contributed to a ROTH TSP.

All FERS employees will receive a 1% automatic agency contribution besides any matched funds. Both these figures are employee benefits and do not increase a participant's income tax, social security tax, or reduce their pay. As the TSP is a long-term retirement account, these two components are vital for a FERS employee's retirement.

The 1% automatic agency contribution is equal to 1% of a FERS employee's basic pay. This amount is given to the

FERS employee by their agency and deposited in the participant's TSP account. However, these funds are subject to vesting, which occurs after a three-year time-in-service for most FERS employees, and is two years for Congressional and certain non-career positions. Any federal civilian service counts towards vesting and not just the service through which the employee participates in the TSP program. A participant's vesting date is based on the TSP Service Computation Date, found on the participant's TSP statements. If a participant leaves government service before vesting, the funds are forfeited. If a FERS employee dies before becoming vested, funds are considered vested on their death.

FERS employees will also receive an agency match of 100% for the first 3% of base pay contributed, and 50% for the next 2% of base pay contributed. Any amount that the participant contributes over the initial 5% does not receive an agency match. Therefore, it makes sense to contribute at least 5% to the TSP as one will receive an additional 4% from the agency. Again, all percentages are based on a participant's base pay. If a participant contributes at least 5% of their base pay to their TSP account, they will receive an additional 5% from their agency, a 4% match, and the 1% automatic agency contribution. CSRS employees and uniformed service members are not eligible for the agency match. The secretary of each service may designate critical specialties as eligible for matching under certain circumstances.

A TSP participant may contribute to the plan based on the IRC and is calculated annually by the IRS. A TSP participant may contribute $17,500, and participants over the age of 50 are allowed a catch-up amount of $5,500. The IRS sets these limits annually, and they may or may not change from year to year. In either case, contribution limits are published on the TSP and IRS websites. The elective deferral limit combines Traditional and ROTH contributions made in a calendar year. For uniformed service members, elective deferral limits are all taxable pay received. The elective deferral limit does not apply to tax-exempt pay earned in a combat zone. For those uniformed service members with a civilian TSP account, the elective deferral limit combines all Traditional and ROTH TSP contributions in all TSP accounts. The 1% automatic agency contribution does not count towards the elective deferral limitations.

For employee contributions, the TSP plan offers two ways for the contributions to be treated. If the participant elects a Traditional TSP contribution, making the contribution before taxes and the participant defers the income tax on that portion of their salary. When withdrawing funds, both the contributions and any gains are taxed as ordinary income to the participant. For uniformed service members who use tax-exempt contributions to fund a Traditional TSP, only the gains are taxed when withdrawing the funds. Participants who make ROTH contributions are electing to pay the taxes on that part of their salary now and not deferring the taxes. Provided the participant meets the requirements to qualify, the gains will be tax-free. Uniformed service members who use tax-exempt contributions to fund a ROTH TSP will also receive tax-free earnings upon their withdrawal.

The difference in the effects of TSP contributions does depend on the tax election the participant chooses. For Traditional TSP contributions, they are deducted from the participant's paycheck before any income is taxed. Using this method lowers the participant's taxable income in the year the contribution was made. Again, all

Thrift Savings Plan: A Practical Guide to the TSP by Kirk G. Meyer

1% automatic agency contributions and agency matches are contributed to a Traditional TSP account. All the participant's proceeds grow in the TSP tax-deferred, and all the withdrawals, participant contributions, agency matching, and taxing any gains as ordinary income. A ROTH TSP contribution is made after the participant's income is already taxed. When withdrawing the funds from a ROTH TSP, both the participant's contributions and any eligible gains will be tax-free. For gains to be considered tax-free, they must have been in the ROTH account for at least five years on January 1 of the calendar year. The participant made the first ROTH contribution, and the participant is at least age 59½, permanently disabled, or deceased. If these criteria are met, the gains will be considered qualified and tax-free.

A tax-exempt contribution is made by a uniformed service member earning tax-exempt pay in a combat zone. If contributions to a Traditional TSP account, the contributions are not taxed, but gains will be taxed as ordinary income. If tax-exempt contributions are made to a ROTH TSP account, both the contributions and gains will be tax-free, provided the criteria mentioned in the previous paragraph are met.

If a participant elects to contribute to a ROTH TSP account, that participant will also have a Traditional TSP account for all agency provided contributions. These two accounts will be maintained separately for tax purposes by the plan's administrators. If a TSP plan participant takes out a loan, makes any withdrawals, or makes inter-fund transfers, taking a proportional amount from each account. And unlike a ROTH individual retirement account where there are income limitations, the ROTH TSP has no such income limitations on participants.

Effect on Taxes between Traditional and ROTH Contributions

When a participant makes a Traditional TSP contribution on a pre-tax basis, there are two general tax advantages. The TSP contribution is not taxed, with both the contribution and the growth thereof being tax-deferred until withdrawn, since the contributions are deducted from the participant's pay before federal and state income taxes being calculated. In this manner, the participant's pay used to calculate taxes is reduced, resulting in less money being withheld in taxes. If the contribution is made to a ROTH TSP with the same percentage, more money will be taken out of the participant's annual take-home pay in theory. With all things being considered equal, the take-home pay between a Traditional TSP and a ROTH TSP is negligible.

If the difference in take-home pay between the Traditional and ROTH TSP is negligible, how does a participant decide which type of TSP is best? The main determining factor that a participant has to decide is whether to be taxed at a higher rate now or later in the retirement years. There is no correct answer to this serious question, but it does come down to the participant's situation and if they require the tax advantages now as compared to later in life. If a participant thinks he will be in the same or higher tax bracket later, it may be better to contribute to a ROTH TSP where all the gains are tax-free. As a general rule of thumb, the breakeven point is the 25% tax bracket.

Many people assume that their tax bracket will be lower in retirement, considering factors before making that assumption. One is, if the participant retires as a FERS employee, she will receive a taxable annuity that is equal to at least 30% of the average of her highest three year's annual base salary, meeting all age and time-in-service requirements. Also, once a participant reaches age 62 and elects to take early social security payments, or even if waiting until full retirement age, a portion of social security benefits may also be taxed if the combination of the annuity payment received in addition to social security benefits causes an excess of income. Now, this is where the tax election will make a difference in retirement assets. If a participant has a Traditional TSP, the entire withdrawal is taxed at the ordinary income tax bracket rate. Considering the participant now has at least two income sources, with one taxed and one partially taxed, any withdrawals from the participant's Traditional TSP will be adding to that taxable income. If a participant makes a large withdrawal, the combination of the three pools of money could cause a fairly high-income tax bracket. However, if the participant elected a ROTH TSP, only a portion of the withdrawals would be added to taxable income, lowering the participant's overall taxable income as compared to the Traditional TSP participant.

Before making any tax elections about the participant's contributions, it is advisable to visit www.tsp.gov and use the Contribution Comparison Calculator. This will allow participants to input their criteria and see the effects on their tax situation. This tool can also project the differences between a Traditional and ROTH TSP regarding the participant's long-term savings. It is also advisable to consult a tax advisor or financial planner if there are issues or questions from the TSP participant. A key point to remember is that anytime the participant's situation changes, modifications can be made to the TSP contribution election between Traditional and ROTH TSP. Only the matching funds are taxed.

Regardless of the contributions of a FERS employee, there will be some tax liability on the Traditional TSP account. With a Traditional TSP, both the contributions and any gains are taxed as ordinary income unless taking certain steps. Provided the participant is eligible, he may put some withdrawals into a traditional individual retirement account or roll the withdrawal into another eligible employer's plan. Provided the taxes are paid on the Traditional TSP's withdrawal in the year they are withdrawn, the balance may be placed into a ROTH individual retirement account. If the participant has a ROTH TSP, the withdrawals from these will not be taxed, since the contributions have been taxed and, provided the gains are qualified, they will be tax-free as well if the participant has gains not qualified, deferring taxes by transferring the payment into a ROTH individual retirement account or another ROTH eligible employer account.

Both TSP plans have an age requirement that must be met before withdrawals are made with no penalty, age 59½. Suppose making a withdrawal before that age, assessing a 10% penalty besides any ordinary income tax. In general, if the participant retires after age 55, she is eligible to make withdrawals from the TSP account with no penalties or additional taxes, provided she has retired with full benefits.

Transferring Funds into a TSP Account

The Traditional TSP allows for transfers and rollovers of tax-deferred funds from traditional individual retirement accounts, SIMPLE IRAs, and other eligible employer plans into the TSP account. TSP will also accept ROTH balance transfers of both qualified and nonqualified ROTH distributions from ROTH 401(k)s, ROTH 403(b)s, and ROTH 457(b)s if the plan participant does not have a ROTH TSP account, created with the transferred funds. The TSP will not accept rollovers of ROTH payments already paid to the participant and rollovers or transfers from ROTH individual retirement accounts.

The participant will now have to decide whether to transfer eligible funds into the TSP account. If the answer to that question is yes, there are two methods to achieve this goal. One is to transfer the money directly from the individual retirement account or employer account directly into the participant's TSP account. To achieve this, use Form TSP-60, Request for a Transfer into the TSP, and Form TSP-60-R for ROTH funds transfers. These two forms are available for download from www.tsp.gov. Suppose the TSP participant wishes to roll over non-ROTH funds directly into the TSP. In that case, they should use Form TSP-60 within 60 days of receiving the funds from an individual retirement account or qualified employer's account. If the TSP participant elects to do a rollover, the former custodian will withhold the appropriate amount for taxes before the money is released. Therefore, if the participant wishes to roll over the entire amount, they add the difference from personal funds to make up for the amount withheld for taxes. Any amount not rolled over is taxed as ordinary income to the participant, in addition to any possible penalties. Any funds added to the participant's TSP will be added according to the latest asset allocation on file with the plan's administrators.

The TSP plan administrators will accept a transfer or a rollover under these conditions: 1. It must be considered an eligible rollover distribution for federal income tax purposes; 2. The participant must have an existing TSP account; and 3. A TSP account cannot be opened with transfer or rollover funds unless it is a ROTH balance transferred into the ROTH TSP account, and a ROTH component does not already exist.

A participant would transfer money into a TSP account to simplify managing accounts and take advantage of the low fees associated with TSP funds. Doing this will make asset management much easier for the participant. With lower fees charged, it will allow the participant's savings to grow faster due to increasing returns and compounding the gains.

Consider that the average actively managed mutual fund may charge up to 1.5%, or even that of a passive indexed exchange-traded fund that may charge 0.1%, over time, the savings of the TSP is 0.039% maximum fund fee. This is an actual savings of up to 1.461%, compared to the actively managed mutual fund, and 0.061% compared to the passive exchange-traded fund. While these figures may not seem very large or significant, let us look at the numbers spread over 30 years. If an active mutual fund earned 6%, an investment of $5,500 would grow to $31,589. A passive exchange-traded fund would earn an adjusted 7.4% return, compared to the mutual fund, due to the savings of management and fund fees of 1.4%, for $46,826 after the same 30 years. As one can see, that is an increase of almost $15,000 just by investing in the passively managed fund. Now, if a participant invested in a TSP fund, she would expect a return of 7.461%, and that same $5,500 would become $47,631 over the same 30 years, which equates to an extra $800 between a low-priced exchange-traded fund and the TSP fund. If one were to contribute money to these funds every year for the entire 30-year period, the extra 0.061% can and will make a difference to a participant's retirement assets.

Allocations and Fees

All TSP participants will be responsible for their asset allocation; however, for participants who do not specify a preference, contributions are invested in the default asset, the G-Fund. The TSP website will allow participants to set their asset allocation by placing a percentage in any of the ten offered funds. TSP's website will also enable participants to do inter-fund transfers twice a month if one moves from the G-Fund into any other fourteen funds. However, a TSP participant may move from the nine funds into the G-Fund at any time. All inter-fund transfers must be submitted by noon Eastern Standard Time on the day the participant wishes the transfer to occur and reflected on the TSP website the following morning.

The asset allocation ability allows the participants of the TSP to invest in a variety of funds discussed later in the booklet. This allocation allows the TSP participant to tell TSP plan administrators where they would like their money invested in their TSP accounts. Plan participants may change the asset allocation at any time, and it will take effect when the participant makes the next contribution deposited. The asset allocation determined by the participant is applied for all funds deposited into the TSP account. Changing the asset allocation will only affect future TSP contributions and will not affect funds already invested. If a plan participant wants to change the asset allocation of funds already deposited, the participant must do an inter-fund transfer instead.

An inter-fund transfer allocates assets already deposited in a participant's TSP account. As one asset increases in value, another may decrease, normally the case with an equity fund and a fixed income fund. As a general rule, an equity fund increases in value, and a fixed-income fund's value will decrease. If these changes in value are significant, it may be necessary for TSP participants to re-allocate their TSP assets to get them back to the desired asset allocation. This is done by logging into the TSP's website and choosing an inter-fund transfer, then simply putting the desired percentages in the corresponding locations. When doing an inter-fund allocation, it is applied to the entire TSP portfolio regardless of its tax allocation benefits. This means the asset allocation will be applied to the Traditional TSP and ROTH TSP, just as participants cannot simply move the funds in one aspect of their TSP account.

Administrative fees associated with the TSP have been historically low compared to mutual funds and many passive exchange-traded funds. The fee charged to plan participants covers the administration of the TSP funds and the costs associated with operating the TSP fund. Some costs include the TSP administrator's recordkeeping fees, participant services, and the printing and mailing of participant statements. The TSP fees are lower than industry averages. One reason the fees are lower is due to forfeitures of the 1% automatic agency contribution associated with FERS employees who leave before becoming vested in the annuity program. Also, other forfeiture fees and loan fees help to offset the TSP administrator's fees.

The ten funds within the TSP have similar administrative fees and have been fairly consistent since 2009. The fee associated with all the TSP funds varies slightly, depending on the fund the participant invests. Current fees associated with TSP funds range from 0.042% in the C-Fund to 0.043% in the F-Fund. Again, this means a cost of $0.43 per $1,000 invested in the F-Fund. These fees are much lower than anything available outside of the TSP, with the lowest priced exchange-traded funds costing about 0.06% for a simple indexed fund such as the S&P 500. When examining the lifecycle funds, they are very inexpensive, with a fee of 0.042% at the most, or $0.42 per $1,000 invested. The L-Fund fees are a weighted average of the funds that make up the L-Fund, which the participant has selected.

Investing and Risks in TSP Funds

Participants of the TSP have two basic choices regarding managing their investment in one or more of the TSP's ten funds. Participants who would like to invest with their retirement year in mind and would like TSP's plan administrators to select the percentages for each asset class can choose the L-Funds or lifecycle funds by selecting a fund that closest matches the participant's retirement year. If the participant wants to invest themself, they can invest in any of the five individual funds available to TSP participants, tied to an index except for the G-Fund, which invests solely in short-term Treasuries issued just for the TSP's G-Fund.

The L-Funds number ten funds, and as one fund reaches its target date, it is retired and will become part of the L-Income fund—the L-Income fund, designed for participants who are retired or are planning to retire before 2020. The next fund is the L-2025 and is in five-year increments out to the year 2065.

While the L-Funds are adequate and do serve a valuable purpose for those participants who would like their TSP account put on "autopilot," I find them to be a little too conservative for today's retirement needs. To see the makeup of an L-Fund, simply go to the TSP website, www.tsp.gov, and select the L-Fund one wishes to research. An example of why these funds are too conservative for someone who may spend 30 plus years in retirement is that the L-Income fund comprises 74% G-Fund and 6% F-Fund, for a total of 80% in bonds. In an environment where bonds are paying higher interest rates, this may not be an issue, but having 80% of one's investments in low yielding bonds may not allow for a 30 plus year retirement. Most financial planners do think that participants, even in retirement, need more exposure to equities to provide for capital appreciation and income. To see another example of how these funds are considered conservative, all one has to do is look at the L-2050 fund, which has 13.5% of the investments in the bond funds. Someone not retiring for at least 30 years can afford to have their entire TSP investment in the equity funds. If a TSP participant uses an L-Fund, I would suggest picking the fund with a target date *after* the one indicated to help combat these funds' conservative nature. As an example, if a TSP participant is scheduled to use the L-2030 fund, they should invest in the L-2040 fund so it will not be as conservative in years where the participant can have more risk in his portfolio. In a later section, the standard deviation of each of the ten non-L-Funds will be examined and explained, as will be the index that the fund tracks.

Before examining each fund, some of the basic risks associated with each TSP fund should be considered. The F-Fund has credit risk, which is the risk that an individual bond cannot pay its interest or principal. The G-Fund is considered not to have any credit risk, as it invests strictly in Treasuries issued by the US government for the G-Fund. The I-Fund and, to some degree, the C-Fund and S-Fund have currency risk associated with each. Concerning the C-Fund and S-Fund, limiting the risk to how much business the individual company has outside the US. The I-Fund has the most currency risk, as the individual stocks may do business in any currency, but at some point, the price of the fund dictates the price be converted to US dollars. All five funds have inflation risk since none is guaranteed to make a return that outpaces inflation. The funds except the G-Fund have market risk, which is the risk that an individual stock or bond will decrease in value due to market conditions. And finally, the F-Fund invests in government and corporate bonds that might have a call feature associated with the bond. If the issuer calls the bond, the fund has prepayment risk as bonds are generally called in an environment where interest rates decline. This poses a risk to the F-Fund because the prepayment of a bond means the fund must reinvest in lower-yielding bonds. Risk in the TSP funds is managed by considering each fund's risk and reward and then investing in funds. By diversifying in different funds, the overall risk of the portfolio is reduced as compared to investing strictly in a single fund, examined when the standard deviation is explained later in the booklet.

Technically, the more time a participant has before she retires, the more risk she should take in these investments. This allows the funds to work over a longer period, with any early losses offset by more gains in later years. All TSP participants need to have an investment strategy to follow. Like any plan, it should be regularly evaluated to ensure the risk and investment strategies are the same as in a previous period. When a participant examines the investment plan, it is good to consider if the assets in the TSP account need to be rebalanced.

Comparison of Funds, Risk/Return, and Diversification

As with any investment, the funds in the TSP need to be researched for the participant's comfort level in the risk versus return of the fund. No investment is without risk in today's investment world. Even US Treasuries have inflation risk, though technically they have no credit risk because the US government has never defaulted on its debt. A general rule accepted in investing is that the more risk an investment has, the greater its return. The TSP funds range from investments with little volatility, or risks like the G-Fund, which also has the lowest standard deviation, to more volatile investments such as the S-Fund and I-Fund, which have higher standard deviations and more risks associated with them.

Volatility is basically how likely investment is to have a wide range of prices. Equities have more volatility than corporate bonds, and US federal government-issued bonds are considered low in volatility. As the price of equity can have large-value changes in a single day, it is considered volatile. Where a bond's value is tied to interest rates and length until maturity, its price can change, but interest rate moves are gradual, over some time. These gradual movements make bond funds less volatile than those made up of equities. Using standard deviation is the likelihood that an investment's price will positively or negatively move away from the mean or average of the securities price. The higher the standard deviation is, the more volatile and risky an investment is. Likewise, the higher an investment's standard deviation is, the higher the return needs to be for the investor annually by spreading risk and volatility over several asset classes or investments, reducing the overall risk and standard deviation for the portfolio as a whole.

The G-Fund is the least volatile fund in the TSP that a participant can invest in. Since the fund is in US Treasuries, it does have a very slight risk associated with it and low volatility. The annualized standard deviation for the G-Fund is 0.3%. The fund has a one-year return of 2.24%, a three-year return of 2.49%, a five-year return of 2.27%, a ten-year return of 2.23%, and a return of about 4.4% since 1990. Considering the average inflation rate has been about 3% based on historical averages, the G-Fund, with its low volatility and standard deviation, produces a return about equal to inflation in the short-term and about 1.5% higher than inflation the last 25 years.

The F-Fund is the next lowest in terms of volatility in the TSP and has the next lowest standard deviation. The F-Fund invests in all kinds of domestic bonds offered in the US that are investment grade. The fund tracks the Barclays Capital US Aggregate Bond Index. The annualized standard deviation for the F-Fund is 3.8%. The fund has a one-year return of 8.68%, a three-year return of 4.6%, a five-year return of 3.25%, a ten-year return of 3.99%, and a return of about 6.1% since 1990. Again, this fund over the short-term has not outpaced the historical inflation rate, but over the last 25 years, it would have an after-inflation return of about 3%. Comparing the two bond funds, it is apparent that there is an added return with the added risk.

The C-Fund is an equity fund that tracks the S&P 500 index and is considered to have moderate volatility. The C-Fund's standard deviation is relatively high at 18.3% and is considered to have moderate volatility by the TSP website. The fund has a one-year return of 15.23%, a three-year return of 12.24%, a five-year return of 14.52%, a ten-year return of 13.66%, and a 10.4% return since 1990. As a TSP participant, one can see where the higher volatility and standard deviation will generally lead to higher returns. The return of the C-Fund outpaces the inflation rate, as will most equity funds. But this added return comes with the price of more volatility and a larger standard deviation, resulting in more risk.

The S-Fund is also an equity fund that invests in small and medium-sized US companies, and it follows the Dow Jones Completion Total Stock Market Index. The S-Fund standard deviation is 20.4%, which is the highest of all the TSP funds. The fund has a one-year return of 12.89%, a three-year return of 8.03%, a five-year return of 11.51%, a ten-year return of 12.21%, and a 10.8% return since 1990 based on the index, as the fund has only existed since 2001. Like the C-Fund, this fund outpaces inflation but is also the most volatile based on its standard deviation and the riskiest.

The last fund is the I-Fund, which invests in established foreign markets and follows the Morgan Stanley Capital International EAFE (Europe, Australia, Far East) Index. This fund's standard deviation is 18.2%, but as shown, this does not reflect on the fund's annualized return. The fund's one-year return is 0.84%, a three-year return of

1.29%, a five-year return of 5.99%, a ten-year return of 4.96%, and a 5.5% return since 1990 based on the index, as the fund has only existed since 2001. The high standard deviation would suggest that the fund's return should be higher for the last 25 years and not less than that of the F-Fund. However, when US markets and securities perform, strong foreign markets can perform in a counter-cyclical manner.

Now that all the funds' standard deviations and returns have been discussed, it is time to see how, by investing in the funds available in the TSP, a plan participant can increase the expected return while decreasing the standard deviation risk. The following portfolios are not suggestions and are not meant to be a financial plan. Rather, they are used as examples of how different asset allocations can achieve higher returns and lower volatility. If a TSP participant put all of his money in the C-Fund, he would have a good annualized return over the last 25 years but would have been exposed to very high volatility based on the standard deviation. And on the other side, had a TSP participant invested 100% in the G-Fund, the returns would have been steady but barely would have beaten inflation.

The key is to find a mixture that a TSP participant feels comfortable regarding risk and potential return. Again, the following are used as examples of how to diversify, increase portfolio return, and decrease the portfolio standard deviation. The following six example portfolios will show the expected annual return and the portfolio's standard deviation, which will be higher than the bond funds and lower than the equity funds. The returns for these sample portfolios react in the same way, by increasing the return over the bond funds and being lower than that of the equity funds. An overall expected return of 8% on all portfolios in these examples.

The first example is to place 20% of a participant's contributions into each of the TSP's five funds. If this is done, the annual return is expected to be 7.43%, with a standard deviation of 8.89%. The return is higher than that of either bond fund but is also more volatile. The added volatility is to compensate the TSP participant for the added risk by investing in equities.

The second and third examples use the three equity funds and switch the two bond funds. If 25% placed in each of the G, C, S, and I-Funds, the expected annual return is 7.55%, with a standard deviation of 10.74%.

Since the participant has increased the investment in riskier equity funds by 5% each, and increasing the G bond fund to 25%, the added risk is resulting in the higher standard deviation, and rewarding the TSP participant with a slightly higher annualized return. The third example takes the 25% in the G-Fund and places it in the riskier F-Fund, with the remaining 75% being placed equally in the three equity funds. In this example, the expected annualized return is 8.99%, and the standard deviation is 11.08%. Here the added risk of the F-Fund increased the standard deviation, and the annualized return. This shows that with added reward, there is added risk. In these examples, the return has increased higher than that of the bond funds individually but is still lower than that of the equity funds; however, the overall volatility of the portfolio is much lower than any one equity fund, showing that by using different asset classes to diversify, reducing volatility.

In the fourth and fifth examples, the portfolios are invested more in the equity funds and less in the bond funds. In the fourth example, the TSP participant would invest 5% each in the F and G-Funds and 30% in each C, S, and I-Funds. In this example, the expected annualized return increases to 9.1%. The standard deviation has increased to 12.92% due to investing in the more volatile equity funds while keeping a small portion in the safest G-Fund. In the fifth example, the TSP participant invests 10% in the F-Fund and 30% in each of the C, S, and I-Funds for an expected annualized return of 9.39% with a standard deviation of 12.99%. The small increases are due to the F-Fund's added risk and return compared to the G-Fund.

In the sixth example, the TSP participant has elected to invest strictly in the equity funds. Based on the facts presented earlier, one should expect a reasonably high return and a high standard deviation, since the equity funds all had standard deviations over 17%. If the TSP contributions are invested equally in the equity funds, the expected annualized return would be 9.64%, with a standard deviation of 14.26%. By diversifying the portfolio, the TSP participant does earn less than the equity funds except for the C and S-funds, but this also decreases what one would have expected for a standard deviation, considering the lowest standard deviation is slightly above 17.8% by itself.

Loans and Withdrawals

As the main purpose of investing in the TSP is to save for retirement, there are certain times in which funds may be taken out of the participant's TSP while still employed. Once an employee leaves service with the federal government, she may take money out of her TSP at any time; however, these withdrawals may be subject to penalties and income tax. There are three ways a TSP participant can take money from a TSP account, and that is through a TSP loan, an in-service withdrawal, and a post-separation withdrawal. Any withdrawal will be taken in equal shares from Traditional and ROTH contributions and being in equal shares from each TSP fund in which the participant has invested.

When a TSP participant takes a loan against a TSP balance, they borrow against contributions already made and any gains achieved. Once the loan is processed, the funds are taken from the participant's TSP account. As the loan is repaid, the participant's TSP account is restored by the loan, in addition to the interest paid on the loan. The interest rate charged to the TSP participant is equal to the interest rate paid on the G-Fund when the loan is taken out. TSP administrators will also impose a $50 fee on each loan to cover the loan processing and its servicing during the life of the loan. This fee is deducted from the total proceeds of the requested loan by the TSP participant.

Interest paid on the loan is not the only cost of taking out a loan against one's TSP account. While the participants repay the loan with interest, they also risk missed opportunities in the funds they were invested in. An example of this is that the fund's price increases, resulting in fewer shares being repurchased as the loan is repaid. But if the price of the fund decreases, the amount of the loan that is paid back will buy more shares. It is not a wise idea for participants to try and time the market in either taking out a loan or in inter-fund transfers. Taking a loan out against TSP funds will reduce the number of shares the participant has in which dividends and interest are paid. Suppose a TSP participant has an outstanding loan when their service with the government is terminated. In that case, they must repay the outstanding balance of the loan in full within 90 days, or penalties and income taxes may be charged against the TSP participant.

Thrift Savings Plan: A Practical Guide to the TSP by Kirk G. Meyer

There are two types of loans allowed through the TSP—a general loan and a real estate loan. A TSP participant may have one loan of each type outstanding at a time but may in no event have more than one of each loan type. The minimum loan processed through the TSP is $1,000, and no more than $50,000 can be borrowed for both loan types combined. The maximum allowed is $50,000, provided the participant has not had an outstanding loan balance in the previous twelve months. If the participant did have an outstanding loan balance, subtracting that amount from the $50,000 maximum. To see the current interest rate for a loan and the amount that a participant can borrow, visit www.tsp.gov, and log into the site using their login information. The site will also estimate the loan payments deducted from each paycheck. The maximum length of a general-purpose loan is five years, while a real estate loan may be repaid over 15 years. These are the maximum lengths allowed, but the participant may elect for shorter loan repayment periods.

There is no documentation required for a general-purpose loan through the TSP. Real estate loans do require some documentation, such as an appraisal.

Check the TSP website to verify what type of documentation is required for a particular real estate loan. There is also a 60-day waiting period between paying off a loan and taking another loan out of the same type. As the repayment of a TSP loan is through payroll deduction, if the participant's agency does not deduct the payment, it is the participant's responsibility to use the TSP Loan Payment Coupon Form TSP-26 to make a payment. A participant with a loan may at any time make a payment or pay off the loan using the same form.

If a TSP participant fails to repay the loan for any reason, it will be considered taxable income and could trigger additional penalties applied to the participant. If the loan comprises ROTH contributions, those will not be taxed, but any gains will be taxed as income. Gains on ROTH contributions do have special tax consequences, so a participant needs to understand that if separation occurs from the government, there are qualified gains that may not be taxed and nonqualified gains, which are taxed as ordinary income. With a loan default, all ROTH gains are taxed whether they are qualified or not. For FERS employees that are married, they must have their spouse's consent to take out a loan, while CSRS employees will have their spouse notified.

For employees, in-service withdrawals are available to all participants. There is no fee for these withdrawals, but they may significantly impact the overall retirement returns and objectives. When an in-service withdrawal happens, the TSP participant will have the proceeds taxed as income, and the withdrawal may be subject to a 10% early withdrawal penalty. If a participant makes an in-service withdrawal, she will be ineligible to contribute for six months. For FERS employees, that means they will lose six months' worth of contributions, and the agency match. There are two types of in-service withdrawals: (1) financial hardship and (2) age-based.

With financial hardship, the participant must certify under the penalty of perjury they are in financial hardship due to negative cash flow, legal expenses in conjunction with a divorce, extreme medical expenses, or personal casualty losses. Participants may withdraw $1,000 or more, but under no circumstance may the withdrawal be more than the financial hardship. An age-based in-service withdrawal occurs when an employee has reached age 59½ and is still in the government's service. In these withdrawals, all or part of the vested amount may be withdrawn for $1,000 or more. If the account has less than $1,000, that amount may be withdrawn. Participants are allowed one age-based in-service withdrawal. If an age-based withdrawal is made, the participant cannot make a partial withdrawal until after separating from government service. FERS employees must have their spouse's consent to make an in-service withdrawal, and with CSRS employees, the spouse will be notified of the in-service withdrawal.

Federal income taxes must be paid on in-service withdrawals when paid directly to the participant owing taxes on the portion taken from the participant's Traditional TSP account. ROTH contributions have been taxed and the gains will be tax-free provided that they are qualified. There will be no taxes withheld in both Traditional and ROTH withdrawals paid to a qualified individual retirement account or an eligible employer plan. ROTH withdrawals must be placed in a ROTH account while Traditional withdrawals can be placed in traditional accounts or converted to ROTH accounts, provided the proper taxes are paid. For financial hardship withdrawals, taxes are assessed based on whether the contributions were Traditional or ROTH, and earnings on Traditional TSP accounts will always be taxed. This is similar to the taxes on an age-based withdrawal. However, in a financial hardship withdrawal, the participant may not have reached the age of 59½ and would be assessed a 10% early withdrawal penalty. For more information on in-service withdrawals, visit www.tsp.gov.

After an employee has separated from government service, withdrawals are allowed, provided a participant has $200 or more vested in the account. Now employees who have separated from government service can leave their funds in the TSP program to take advantage of the extremely low administrative fees. Participants may also elect to move a portion of their funds to other qualified individual retirement accounts or employer plans. If a participant separates from the government, they must keep a current address on file with TSP administrators for plan communications. If a participant's TSP account balance that is vested is less than $200, TSP will send the participant a check for the amount.

If a participant is a civilian and uniformed service member after separating from one, it is possible to combine accounts. When accounts are combined, Traditional balances are placed in Traditional accounts, while ROTH balances are transferred to ROTH accounts. These transfers will occur following the same asset allocations of the original TSP account. If the account transferred has an outstanding loan, the loan must be repaid in full before the transfer can occur. TSP accounts that contain tax-exempt contributions can only be transferred if they are contained in a ROTH account, and if they are in a Traditional account, they must remain in separate TSP accounts and cannot be combined.

There are two types of post-separation withdrawals, those being partial withdrawals or full withdrawals. A partial withdrawal allows a participant to take out $1,000 or more, leaving the account's remainder intact for later use. A participant may make only one partial withdrawal, and if he has made an age-based withdrawal, he is ineligible for a partial withdrawal. A full withdrawal is a withdrawal intended to exhaust the TSP account and done using one or a combination of three options. Full withdrawals may be accomplished by taking a single lump sum, creating a series of monthly payments made to the participant by TSP, or purchasing a life annuity for the participant through TSP plan administrators. The lump sum or single payment will pay the participant the entire amount in the TSP account at one time. When a lump sum payment is taken, taxes on the full amount are owed in the year payment on the lump sum was made.

TSP participants who decide on monthly payments can tell TSP a dollar amount they wish to receive until the funds are exhausted. A second option for monthly payments is to have TSP administrators calculate a monthly payment based on the participant's life expectancy. If the participant chooses a specific dollar amount, it must be at least $25 per month. When a participant chooses payments, there are several options available. First, at any time, a participant may ask TSP to stop the payments and make a lump sum payment. Second, participants who receive monthly payments may also ask TSP to change their payments once a year. And finally, participants who had TSP calculate their monthly payment based on their life expectancy have one opportunity to switch to a fixed payment they select. An advantage of taking monthly payments is taxes are spread over months and years, instead of being due at one time as in a lump sum payment.

If the TSP participant decides on an annuity, payments are received as long as they live and even for the spouse's life if the participant dies first. TSP plan administrators will purchase the annuity on the participant's behalf from a private insurance company. The annuity may be purchased with all or a portion of the funds available in the TSP when the full withdrawal is requested. As a general rule, funding an annuity must be with $3,500 or more. If a life annuity is selected, the participant must have a balance in only one type of TSP account, Traditional or ROTH. For those participants who have both a Traditional and ROTH TSP account, provided they have $3,500 in each account, two annuities of the same type will be purchased. If a participant elects to use 100% of her TSP funds to purchase an annuity, $3,500 must be available in each type of TSP account. If, for some reason, a participant has TSP accounts, and only one has a balance of over $3,500, the other account will be closed and a check sent to the participant. If using an annuity as part of a mixed withdrawal, any amounts not used to purchase the requested annuity will be split and distributed according to the other withdrawal options selected.

There are three basic annuity types that the TSP plan administrators offer. The first is a single-life annuity, which will pay only the participant for their lifetime with no benefits to a surviving spouse. A second option is a joint-life annuity with the participant's spouse. This annuity will pay the participant and spouse for both of their lifetimes so that when one spouse dies, the payments will continue for the other. The monthly payments for this annuity will be lower than the single life product because there is a greater chance the payments will last longer. The third annuity option is a joint-life annuity with the survivor being someone other than a spouse. This person, however, must have an insurable interest in the TSP participant. This annuity works the same as the second, paying benefits for the life of both the participant and the second person named in the annuity contract. If a joint annuity is selected, the participant may choose between a 50% and 100% payment option to the survivor. The lower the percentage paid to the survivor, the higher the participant's payment will be while alive. The TSP offers variations on the basic annuity. For more information on the annuities, visit the TSP website at www.tsp.gov.

Once an employee has separated from federal government service, he must begin to withdraw from his TSP account by April 1 of the year following the year he reaches age 72. If an employee is past the age of 72 and is still in the government's service, he does not have to withdraw until April 1 of the year after terminating employment with the government. If one misses the established deadline and does not make withdrawals, the TSP account will be forfeited to TSP. These forfeited accounts may be reclaimed, but the participant will receive no future gains on a forfeited account. The IRS also imposes minimum distributions on TSP participants, which dictate the amount that must be withdrawn based on the participant's life expectancy. For more information on minimum withdrawals, visit www.tsp.gov or www.irs.gov.

Death Benefits

If the death of a TSP participant occurs who has designated a beneficiary or beneficiaries, distributing the funds in the TSP account in the manner outlined in the beneficiary designation is done. If a participant does not name a beneficiary, the funds will be distributed to the following as prescribed by local laws where the participant died. If no beneficiary is named, the TSP plan administrators will first distribute to the spouse, followed by the participant's child, children, or descendants of deceased children, followed by parents or parent, followed by the administrator or executor of the estate, and finally, the next of kin as determined under the laws of the state in which the participant lived at the time of death.

As a participant, name a beneficiary to avoid the issues discussed above. By naming a beneficiary, many issues are avoided, and the participant will ensure the person of his or her choice will receive the proceeds of the TSP. To name a beneficiary, use Form TSP-3. For the form to be legal, it must be signed, witnessed, and received by TSP by the date of the participant's death. If a participant is divorced from the spouse named as the beneficiary, the divorced spouse will still receive the proceeds of the TSP unless the participant formally changes beneficiary. Keep named beneficiaries up to date to ensure the proper people will benefit from the participant's death and not a former spouse unless that is the intention.

For beneficiaries to receive the TSP account's death benefits, they or their representative must submit Form TSP-17 for civilian accounts and Form TSP-U-17 for uniformed service members. These forms should be sent to TSP administrators, along with information on the deceased participant and a certified death certificate. Once TSP has received the required information, they will contact the beneficiaries with further instructions and provide them with additional information. For more information on beneficiaries and death benefits, visit www.tsp.gov.

When a TSP participant dies, the beneficiary may have a beneficiary account with TSP, provided the amount at the time of the participant's death was greater than $200. When this occurs, a beneficiary account is established, and invest all the available TSP funds in the

G-Fund. As a beneficiary, there are a few options available, which are to leave the funds in the TSP account and manage them, combine the proceeds into their TSP account (provided the beneficiary is in the service of the federal government), or withdraw the funds in a manner discussed earlier in the booklet.

TSP Beneficiaries

When a TSP participant dies, their TSP account is disbursed according to the Form TSP-3 filled out by designating a beneficiary or beneficiaries. If the TSP account has more than $200, a new TSP account will be created in the beneficiary's name. At that point, they are issuing a welcome letter to the new owners of the TSP account. This letter will contain the new owner's thirteen-digit account number and any identifying information that the TSP administrators have on the new owner. This information must be verified for accuracy. If any errors are present, notify the TSP administrators immediately.

Beneficiary owners of TSP accounts cannot make contributions, take out loans against the TSP funds, or transfer any money into the TSP account. A beneficiary owner will enjoy the TSP's low administrative fees and name her beneficiary for the TSP account with those exceptions. If the new owner does have an existing TSP account, the two can be combined into one account, and the funds left in the TSP account with several withdrawal options.

As a new TSP owner, the beneficiary must establish an online account with the thirteen-digit account number at www.tsp.gov. This will allow the owner to adjust the asset allocation, as all funds are automatically placed in the G-Fund upon the original TSP participant's death. Once a new owner receives a unique eight-character password and four-digit PIN, he will be allowed the online access needed to manage his account. As of 2020, the TSP website now requires a two-form authentication process to obtain entry. If the account login or password is forgotten at any time, a new one is mailed to the owner through the US Postal Service, generally delivered to the owner within ten days of the request.

In the event of the new TSP owner's death, the funds cannot remain in the TSP account and distribute to all beneficiaries named on the Form TSP-3 completed by the new owner. These funds can be distributed to individuals, trusts, or other entities that the owner wishes to receive the funds. It is also noted that if a TSP beneficiary maintains the TSP account, upon their death, the funds must be distributed as cash and cannot roll over into an individual retirement account (Traditional or

Thrift Savings Plan: A Practical Guide to the TSP by Kirk G. Meyer

ROTH), as an inherited individual retirement account, or into an employer plan.

When a beneficiary TSP owner designates their beneficiary, TSP plan administrators will notify the owner through the mail. If there is an error in a beneficiary designation, the TSP administrators will notify the owner of any errors that will need to be corrected before naming the beneficiary legally. If an owner does not name a beneficiary, the order of precedence is the same as if it were the original TSP participant. As a new owner, the participant designates a new beneficiary because a will does not affect the TSP funds. Just as an original TSP participant, it is important for any new owners to keep beneficiary information up to date to ensure proper disposition of the assets.

As a beneficiary owner, the first quarterly statement is mailed to the new owner. If the new owner wishes to continue to receive statements in the mail, they must do so by logging into the TSP website and making the request. The statement will also be mailed on a calendar year basis to the owner so he/she can monitor the TSP account. All TSP owners need to check their statements to ensure they are accurate. Particularly, make sure the name, address, and date of birth are correct. If there were any transactions during the period, make sure they are correct.

If, as a new owner, the beneficiary already has a personal TSP account, the accounts may be combined, with the additional funds being treated as employee contributions but not subject to IRS limitations. If the TSP account inherited contains tax-exempt money, that portion may not be transferred into a civilian account. If the owner combines the accounts, the tax-exempt funds will be paid to the owner unless the tax-exempt funds were placed in a ROTH TSP account and, therefore, allowed to transfer into a ROTH TSP account for the new owner. As for determining the ROTH initiation date, it is the earlier of the two accounts if both the owner and the original TSP participant had them. It will be the original owner's date in the event the new owner does not have a ROTH TSP component. To combine TSP accounts, the new owner must fill out and submit Form TSP-90, Withdrawal Request for Beneficiary Participants.

Unique Rules for Uniformed Service Members

Unlike civilian government employees, uniformed service members are eligible for retirement benefits for as little as two years of service, or if they put in their full 20 years and reach their full retirement benefits. If a uniformed service member receives tax-exempt combat pay and places those funds in a ROTH TSP account, the benefits should add up to a very nice tax-free lump sum for retirement years. And unlike civilian employees, uniformed service members can elect to contribute not only a portion of their basic pay, but their tax-exempt pay, incentive pay, special pay, and bonus pay.

Name and Form Numbers of Useful Forms

Form TSP-1 Thrift Savings Plan Election Form. This form establishes a civilian participant's desire to either contribute to a TSP account or elect to stop all TSP contributions.

Form TSP-U-1 Thrift Savings Plan Election Form. This form establishes a uniformed service member's desire to either contribute to a TSP account or elect to stop all TSP contributions.

Form TSP-1-C Thrift Savings Plan Catch-Up Contribution Election. This is the form used by those over the age of 50 who wish to make catch-up contributions.

Form TSP-3 Designation of Beneficiary. This form allows the TSP participant to designate primary and contingent beneficiaries if the participant's death occurs.

Form TSP-9 Change in Address Form for Separated Participants. This allows those who have separated from government service to change their official address.

Form TSP-15 Change in Name Form for Separated Participants. This allows those who have separated from government service to change their legal name on their TSP account.

Form TSP-20 Loan Application. This is the form that a participant needs to fill out and submit to the TSP administrators to take out a loan against a TSP account.

Form TSP-26 Loan Payment Coupon. This is the form that must accompany a loan payment made through means other than a payroll deduction.

Form TSP-60 Request for a Transfer into the TSP. This form allows a participant to transfer eligible funds into an existing TSP account.

Form TSP-70 Request for Full Withdrawal. This is the form a participant needs to fill out and submit when requesting a full withdrawal of TSP funds.

Form TSP-73 Change in Monthly Payment Amount. This is the form required if a participant wishes to change the monthly payment amount.

These forms and other TSP forms and information may be found on the TSP website, www.tsp.gov.

About Kirk G. Meyer

Kirk G. Meyer's educational and work background is relatively diverse. Kirk is working on his Doctorate in Business Administration from William Howard Taft University. Kirk has completed an MS in Financial Planning from Bentley University in suburban Boston, Massachusetts, and is now a Registered Financial Consultant in the State of Tennessee and working for the government in contracts. Kirk also holds an MBA and MS in Accounting from Strayer University in Washington, DC, and a BS in Business Administration from Haskell Indian Nations University in Lawrence, Kansas.

Before Kirk's current position with the federal government in contracts, he was a bank examiner for a federal regulatory agency. Besides Kirk's education and work experience, he is a licensed independent financial planner and licensed to sell life insurance and annuities in his home state of Tennessee, advising on these and other financial matters and products to individuals and families in need while performing his duties as a financial planner. Kirk's educational background and love of helping others make him an asset to those looking for assistance and guidance in financial and personal finance matters. Kirk resides in Nashville, Tennessee, with his lovely wife.

How to Contact Kirk G. Meyer

Email Kirk at kirk@kgmeyerpc.com.

Please follow Kirk's blog at www.kgmeyerpc.com, and he welcomes any comments or suggestions on how to make his blog or eBooks better for you.

You can also follow Kirk on Twitter at @kirkgmeyer

You can follow Kirk on Facebook at www.facebook.com/kgmeyerpc

You can follow Kirk on LinkedIn at www.linkedin.com/in/kirkgmeyer

Kirk can also be found on www.goodreads.com/kirkgmeyer.

One Last Chance for the Free Gifts!

Again, as a big thank you for getting *Thrift Savings Plan: A Practical Guide to the TSP*, I want to offer you some valuable gifts and a chance to get some on-going financial advice. Just for getting this book, it entitles you to my Budget Spreadsheet and Debt Reduction Spreadsheet that I normally sell for $10. It is yours free for getting *Thrift Savings Plan: A Practical Guide to the TSP* and signing up for my free email newsletters that have previews to my eBooks. These special articles are geared towards personal finance and now access to these two useful spreadsheets. To get your spreadsheets now, go to my blog's website and sign up today. Visit http://bit.ly/KGMLetter today to get your free valuable spreadsheets.

Other Books by Kirk G. Meyer

Thrift Savings Plan: A Practical Guide to the TSP

The Basics of Life Insurance

A Brief Overview of Annuities

Financial Plans: Just the Basics

Personal Finance: A Grouping of Financial Topics

Final Expense Insurance

Budgeting 101

The Basics of Life Insurance and Annuities Bundle

Your Credit Report and You

The Basics of Personal Finance

Investing 101: A Basic Guide to Investing for Beginners

How the Stock Market Operates

401(k) Retirement Loans

Basic Personal Finance: How to Maintain a Financial Strategy

101 Powerful Tips for Legally Improving Your Credit Score